J
536

Barratt, D   H
  Heat

DATE DUE

HILLSIDE PUBLIC LIBRARY

HILLSIDE, ILLINOIS

DEMCO

Discovering Science

heat

D. H. BARRATT

Illustrated by Advertising Artists Leeds and C. Instrell

WORLD PUBLISHING

TIMES MIRROR

NEW YORK

CONTENTS

Published 1972 by The World Publishing Company
Library of Congress Catalog Card Number: 79–184849
ISBN 0–529–04606–7; 0–529–04607–5
(Trade edition)   (Library edition)
© 1963; © 1969 revised edition,
E. J. Arnold & Son Limited
All rights reserved
Printed in Great Britain by E. J. Arnold & Son Limited, Leeds

WORLD PUBLISHING
TIMES MIRROR

Chapter 1

Solids, liquids and gases

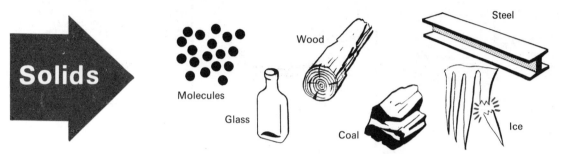

Solids

Molecules

Glass

Wood

Coal

Steel

Ice

Everything in the world is made up of millions and millions of very tiny particles called **molecules.** A molecule is so tiny that thousands would be needed to cover a pin head. In some things the molecules are close together. These things are called **solids**. A solid has a shape of its own.

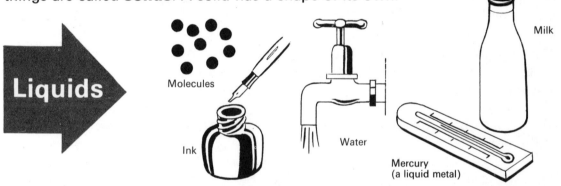

Liquids

Molecules

Ink

Water

Milk

Mercury
(a liquid metal)

In some things the molecules are further apart. These things are called **liquids**. A liquid takes the shape of the container it is kept in. It has to be kept in a container made of a solid to stop it from running away.

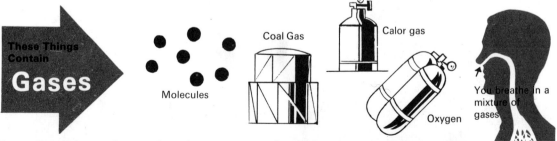

These Things Contain

Gases

Molecules

Coal Gas

Calor gas

Oxygen

You breathe in a mixture of gases

In some things the molecules are even further apart, and these things are called **gases**. Most gases cannot be seen, but some can be smelt. A gas has no shape of its own. A gas is sometimes kept in a container made of a solid to stop it from escaping into the air.

The molecules of solids, liquids and gases are always moving. The hotter a thing becomes, the faster the molecules move.

SOLID

A block of ice

LIQUID

When the ice is heated, the molecules move more quickly and become further apart. The ice becomes water.

GAS

When heating continues, the molecules move more quickly still, and some of the liquid becomes a gas.

Look at the picture of a **solid** block of ice. The molecules are close together but they shake. If you heat the ice, the molecules begin to shake faster, moving further and further apart until the ice shakes apart and becomes a **liquid**—water. We say ice **melts**.

If you go on heating the water, the molecules move so fast that some jump right out of the water into the air. Water becomes a **gas**—water vapor. We say water **evaporates**.

Many solids become liquids if we heat them enough. There are some examples in the drawings.

Very hot rock becomes liquid and turns into lava

lava

lava

Solid ice-cream melts into a liquid

Hot liquid metal is poured into a mould

Heated liquids change into gases; often the gas can be smelled. When a solid melts, it takes heat from the things around it. When snow and ice melt they take heat from the air. That is why it often feels so cold during a thaw.

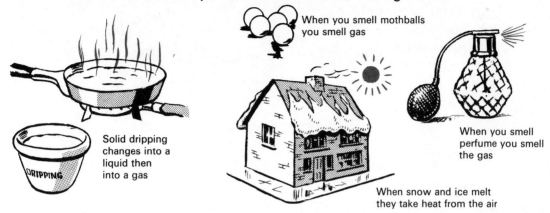

Solid dripping changes into a liquid then into a gas

When you smell mothballs you smell gas

When you smell perfume you smell the gas

When snow and ice melt they take heat from the air

When a liquid **evaporates** it takes heat from the things around it. Wet the back of your hand. Your hand begins to feel cold as the water evaporates. This is why it is foolish to sit about in damp clothes or in damp shoes and socks.

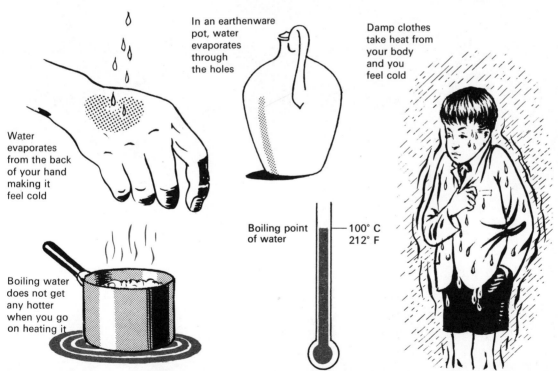

Water evaporates from the back of your hand making it feel cold

In an earthenware pot, water evaporates through the holes

Damp clothes take heat from your body and you feel cold

Boiling water does not get any hotter when you go on heating it

Boiling point of water — 100° C 212° F

Milk and butter coolers work because evaporating water keeps them cool. When you go on heating boiling water, the water does not get any hotter; the heat is used to change the water into water vapor.

Most solids when heated become liquids, then gases. Some solids become **gases** when heated.

What happens if you **cool** a gas? When you cool water vapor it changes or **condenses** into water. When most gases are cooled they become liquids.

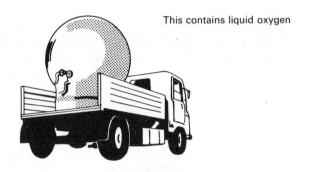

This contains liquid oxygen

Scientists can make liquid air. You sometimes see huge globes filled with liquid oxygen on trucks. (Oxygen is one of the gases in the air.)

Water vapor.
This cools again
to become
water

You breathe out
carbon dioxide

Liquid
carbon
dioxide
is used by
firemen to
put out fires

One of the gases you breathe out, **carbon dioxide**, is carried as a liquid in canisters by firemen who use it for putting out fires.

If you cool a **liquid** it becomes a solid—if water is cooled it becomes **ice**.

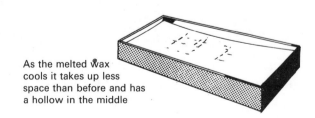

As the melted wax
cools it takes up less
space than before and has
a hollow in the middle

6

A dish of melted wax appears as in the drawing on page 6. After it has cooled, the solid wax takes up less room than liquid wax. Most things get **smaller** when they cool from a liquid to a solid.

When plastic is moulded there is so much shrinkage in the solid state that a mould has to be made with the sides bulging out so that when the plastic cools an accurate shape is formed.

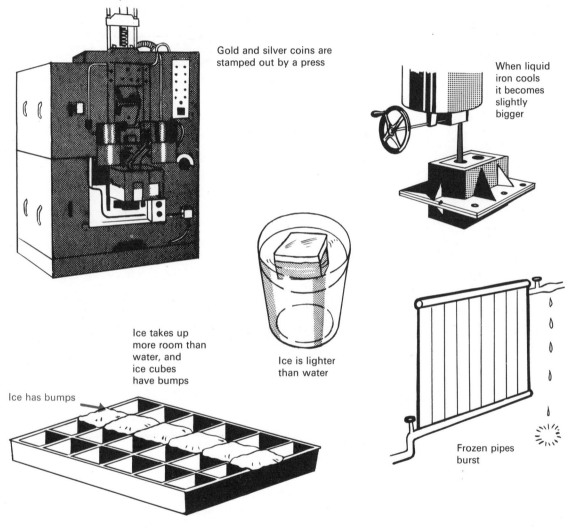

Gold and silver coins are stamped out by a press

When liquid iron cools it becomes slightly bigger

Ice takes up more room than water, and ice cubes have bumps

Ice is lighter than water

Ice has bumps

Frozen pipes burst

Iron can be moulded because when liquid iron cools it becomes slightly bigger. Ice cubes coming from a fridge have 'bumps', as in the picture, because ice takes up more room than water. That is why frozen pipes and radiators burst and why water freezing in the cracks in rocks breaks up the rock.

Ice is lighter than water: an ice cube floats in a jug of water, and icebergs float in the sea.

7

Chapter 2

Expansion and contraction

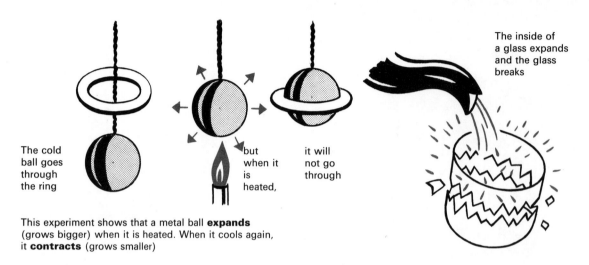

The cold ball goes through the ring

but when it is heated,

it will not go through

The inside of a glass expands and the glass breaks

This experiment shows that a metal ball **expands** (grows bigger) when it is heated. When it cools again, it **contracts** (grows smaller)

You know now that when something is heated, its molecules move about more quickly and push away from each other, making more room for themselves.

Things **expand** when they are heated and **contract** when they cool.

This is important in the home. A metal screw top which is stuck on a bottle can be removed if you run hot water over the top for a few minutes. It then unscrews easily because the heat has made the metal top expand.

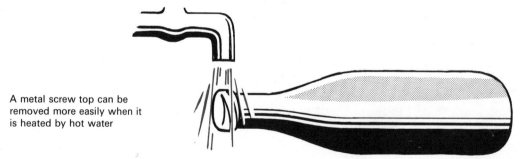

A metal screw top can be removed more easily when it is heated by hot water

Boiling water breaks a milk bottle or thick glass tumbler because the inside of the glass expands more than the outside. Specially toughened glass is made so that it does not crack when heated.

The knowledge is also important in engineering and industry. Engineers must remember that some things, when heated, expand more than others. Zinc and aluminum, for example, expand more than copper or steel; cement expands more than steel; pyrex glass expands about half as much as ordinary glass.

HEAT

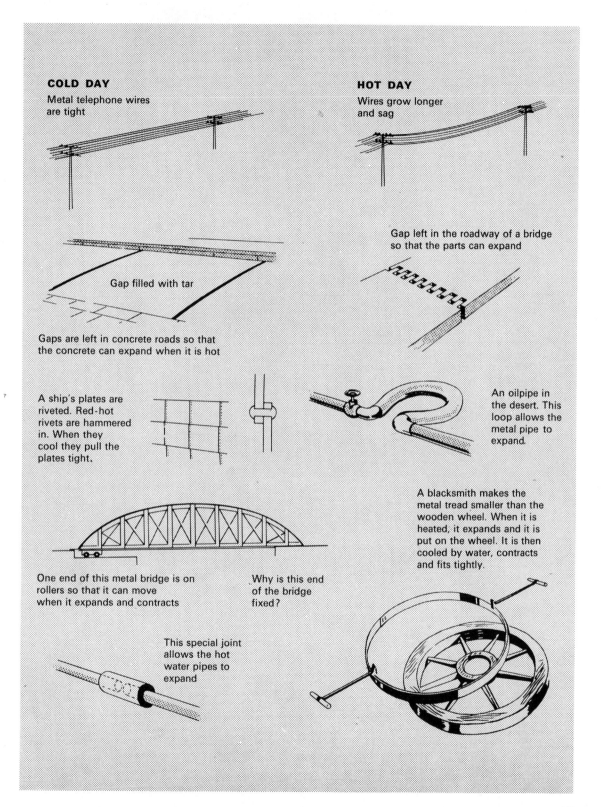

COLD DAY
Metal telephone wires
are tight

HOT DAY
Wires grow longer
and sag

Gap left in the roadway of a bridge
so that the parts can expand

Gap filled with tar

Gaps are left in concrete roads so that
the concrete can expand when it is hot

A ship's plates are
riveted. Red-hot
rivets are hammered
in. When they
cool they pull the
plates tight.

An oilpipe in
the desert. This
loop allows the
metal pipe to
expand.

A blacksmith makes the
metal tread smaller than the
wooden wheel. When it is
heated, it expands and it is
put on the wheel. It is then
cooled by water, contracts
and fits tightly.

One end of this metal bridge is on
rollers so that it can move
when it expands and contracts

Why is this end
of the bridge
fixed?

This special joint
allows the hot
water pipes to
expand

The saucepan in the first picture is filled right to the brim with cold water. When it is heated some of the water spills over the edge. This proves that liquids **expand** when heated.

When it has cooled down, however, the water does not fill the saucepan. This means that liquids **contract** when cooled down.

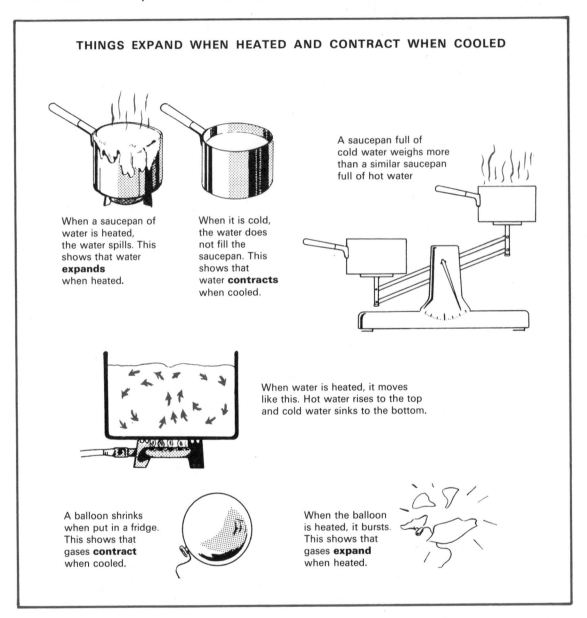

THINGS EXPAND WHEN HEATED AND CONTRACT WHEN COOLED

When a saucepan of water is heated, the water spills. This shows that water **expands** when heated.

When it is cold, the water does not fill the saucepan. This shows that water **contracts** when cooled.

A saucepan full of cold water weighs more than a similar saucepan full of hot water

When water is heated, it moves like this. Hot water rises to the top and cold water sinks to the bottom.

A balloon shrinks when put in a fridge. This shows that gases **contract** when cooled.

When the balloon is heated, it bursts. This shows that gases **expand** when heated.

Can you see from the picture above that a saucepan full of hot water will weigh less than one full of cold water? This shows us that hot water is lighter than cold water.

10

HEAT

A Frenchman called Montgolfier one day noticed his mother's skirt, which was drying above the fire, billow upwards towards the ceiling. This gave him an idea and he thought that a hot air balloon would rise into the air.

When gunpowder burns, gases are given off. These expand suddenly because of the heat and thrust a rocket into the air, as you see in the drawing.

MONTGOLFIER'S BALLOON

Fire

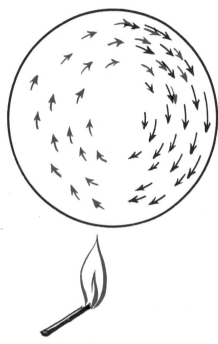

Hot air is lighter than cold air. When it is heated, it moves like this. Hot air rises and cold air takes the place of the hot air

In an explosion, expanding gases push over the walls of the buildings and break the windows

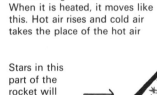

Stars in this part of the rocket will burst out when it is set on fire

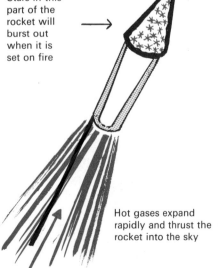

Hot gases expand rapidly and thrust the rocket into the sky

Chapter 3

How heat is produced 1

When it cools, it becomes black again

A black iron poker becomes red hot in a fire

A piece of burning paper can be put out if you put your foot on it

Put one end of a cold black iron poker in the fire until it is red hot, then take it out. It cools and becomes a cold black iron poker again.

If you put one end of a piece of paper in the fire, then take it out, it goes on giving off heat. The black stuff that is left does not look like paper. What has happened? As the paper gets hot, it joins with **oxygen** (a gas that is in the air) and changes into something else. **As it changes it gives off heat.** You can feel the heat and you can **see** the flame as the paper **burns**. The flame goes out when no more of the paper will join with oxygen.

You can stop the paper burning if you put your foot on it. This stops oxygen from getting to the paper.

If you blow gently, it will burn more quickly

Blow hard to blow it out

You can blow the flame out. When you blow you cool the paper so that there is not enough heat to change the paper to a gas. If you blow gently, you blow more oxygen onto the paper and it burns more fiercely.

12

Many things in the world will burn. Some need only a very small amount of heat. We say they are **inflammable**.

The pictures show some things which are so inflammable that they are dangerous.

Notices like the ones shown are used to warn us that certain things are dangerous. Many materials are treated in a special way so that they do not burn easily. Very rapid burning in a small space can cause an explosion.

Some dangerous explosives are shown in the pictures.

Methylated Spirit

Fat or oils used for deep-frying

NOTICES LIKE THESE WARN US THAT GASOLINE AND OTHER INFLAMMABLE LIQUIDS ARE DANGEROUS

NO SMOKING
INFLAMMABLE

DANGER
PLEASE SWITCH OFF YOUR ENGINE

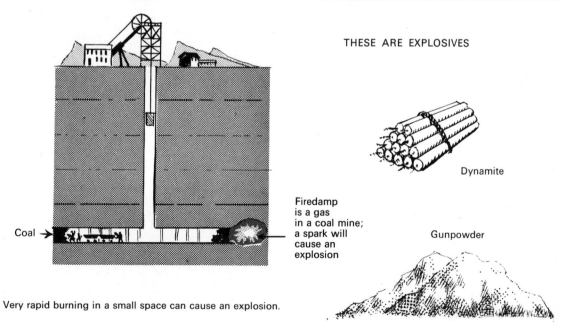

THESE ARE EXPLOSIVES

Dynamite

Gunpowder

Coal →

Firedamp is a gas in a coal mine; a spark will cause an explosion

Very rapid burning in a small space can cause an explosion.

Some things need a great deal of heat to make them burn. A diamond changes into carbon dioxide in great heat. But some things will not burn at all, such as water, sand and chalk.

Water

Chalk

Sand

These things burn easily to give us heat. They are fuels. They were once living plants or animals.

Wood

Coal

Paper

Oil

Gas

About 250 million years ago the land was covered with strange fern-like trees growing in hot, steamy swamps. When these trees died, they fell into the swamp and rock formed over them. The trees were pressed by the weight above them and coal was formed.

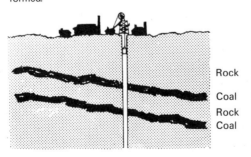

Rock
Coal
Rock
Coal

Later in time, many tiny animals and plants lived in shallow seas. When they died, they fell to the bottom of the sea and rock formed above them, pressing them down to form oil.

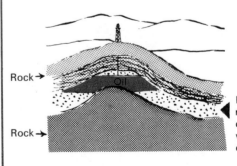

Rock →

Oil

Rock →

Porous rock (lets oil and water collect)

Have you ever picked up a charred piece of wood?

It is mainly **carbon**. All living things—plants and animals—contain carbon, so all **fuels** contain carbon. When fuels burn, the carbon joins the oxygen in the air to make other gases. One is **carbon dioxide**.

Match

Paper

Small coal

Large coal

Thin sticks

Large sticks

The sticks should be laid like this

To make a fire burn more brightly we can push a poker in to lift the coal . . .

. . . or open the front to let more oxygen into the fire

When we want a fire to burn more slowly, we heap slack on it and close the front to stop air flowing through it

To make a fire you must have **fuel**, **oxygen** and enough **heat** to start the **fuel** burning. You can make a coal fire with a match, sticks, paper and coal because the pink end of the match needs a very small amount of heat to make it burn. This makes the paper burn, the paper sets fire to the wood and finally the coal begins to burn. You use thin sticks and little pieces of coal because tiny pieces burn more easily than big ones. You lay the fire as you see in the drawing so that air can get to the middle of it.

CHIMNEYS, FUNNELS AND BELLOWS
CAUSE A GOOD DRAFT OF AIR
THROUGH A FIRE

TO PUT OUT A FIRE, YOU STOP
THE AIR REACHING IT . . .

If you see smoke coming
from a building, 'phone
the fire department. Do
not open the door.

Cover on
a lighter

A person who is on
fire should be
rolled in a
rug

Candle snuffer

. . . OR COVER THE
FLAMES WITH
SOMETHING
THAT WILL NOT
BURN

Use water

Throw sand on the fire

Cover the
fire with
foam or a
fine spray
from a
fire
extinguisher

16

Chapter 4

How heat is produced 2

Quicklime
will burn
your hands

Heat is made when
cement is
being made

CEMENT

Heat is made when a substance joins with oxygen and changes into something different.

But the heat is also made when things change in other ways. Your hands get hot if you touch quicklime when they are wet because when quicklime is mixed with water it changes into a different kind of lime ('slaked lime') and heat is made. When powders that make cement are mixed with water the mixture becomes warm because one of the powders is quicklime.

Manure heaps
become hot enough
to incubate grass
snake's eggs

Fire is sometimes caused in a hayrick when damp hay decays

If a hay rick is made of damp hay, the hay starts to decay and change. The middle of a damp hay rick can become so hot that it catches fire. The farmer must be very careful to dry the hay before he stacks it.

The middle of a manure heap gets quite hot, and grass snakes often lay their eggs in manure heaps. The heat incubates and hatches the eggs.

17

There is a story of a country doctor who was once called to examine a little boy with measles. When he arrived at the farm-house he could not see Jimmy, but he could smell a manure heap in the corner of the room. Then he noticed Jimmy's head sticking out of the top of the heap. "Will our Jimmy be all right?" asked his mother. The doctor had to admit that the manure kept the boy as warm as two or three hot water bottles and an eider-down.

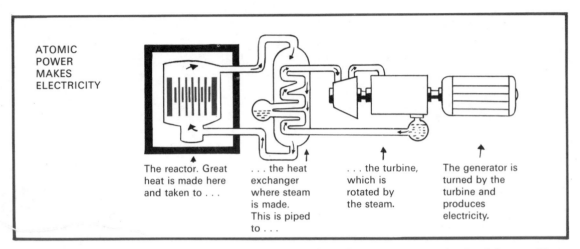

ATOMIC POWER MAKES ELECTRICITY

The reactor. Great heat is made here and taken to . . .

. . . the heat exchanger where steam is made. This is piped to . . .

. . . the turbine, which is rotated by the steam.

The generator is turned by the turbine and produces electricity.

Scientists have now found another way of making a great deal of heat. They change the atoms of one thing into the atoms of another. In atomic reactors atoms of a metal called uranium are changed into atoms of something else. Great heat is made. This heat is used to turn water into steam to drive turbines. Some of these turbines drive generators in electric power stations. Some turbines drive submarines and nuclear merchant ships.

Terrific heat is released in a hydrogen bomb explosion

The terrific heat and great explosion of an atomic or hydrogen bomb are caused by atoms changing into other atoms. When a hydrogen bomb explodes, the atoms of hydrogen are changed to atoms of helium—another gas.

The heat from a hydrogen bomb is very small compared to the heat of the sun. There, four million tons of hydrogen are changed into helium **every second**. When all the hydrogen is changed, the sun will go cold and life will end on our earth. That need not worry you, because scientists tell us that there is enough hydrogen for the sun to give heat for millions more years. You can see from the diagram that only a very small part of the sun's heat reaches our earth.

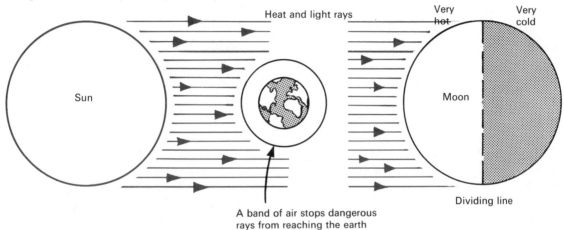

Heat and light rays

Very hot

Very cold

Sun

Moon

Dividing line

A band of air stops dangerous rays from reaching the earth

Just as an atom bomb gives out dangerous rays, so also does the sun. Fortunately for us, the band of air round the earth prevents most of these rays from reaching us. This band of air stops quite a lot of heat too.

A man wears a space suit on the moon to protect himself from dangerous rays and heat and cold

When the first man landed on the moon, which has no air round it, he had to be protected from these dangerous rays and from great heat and cold. When the sun shines on the moon, the surface of the moon becomes hotter than our hottest deserts and yet, minutes after the sun has set, it becomes colder than the North Pole. The place where man landed on the moon was named The Sea of Tranquility.

When you strike a match, where does the heat come from that makes it burn?

Rub your hand on the corner of the desk. Your hand feels hot. You can 'burn' your hand as you slide down a rope. If you rub a soft duster over a rough piece of wood, the wood drags little pieces from the duster. When any two surfaces rub together they drag against each other and this makes heat. We call this drag **friction**.

The rougher the surfaces the more friction there is. Two rough surfaces rubbed very quickly against each other make enough heat to start a fire. Primitive tribes use this method. In a tinder box and cigarette lighter the spark made by rubbing falls on something that catches fire easily (thin shavings of wood or a fluid-soaked wick). The heat made when the pink end of a match is rubbed against the rough end of the match box sets fire to the chemicals on the end of the match.

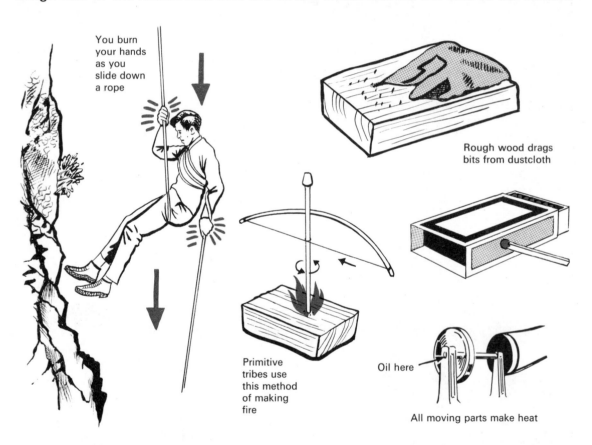

You burn your hands as you slide down a rope

Rough wood drags bits from dustcloth

Primitive tribes use this method of making fire

Oil here

All moving parts make heat

When the brakes of a car are used a lot, the brake drums become hot because of friction. In machines with wheels or moving parts, too much heat would stop the machine from working; therefore all the surfaces are made very smooth and all parts are oiled. This means that there is very little friction, so there is very little heat.

Heat is made when one thing changes into another: when a fire burns, a hayrick decays, when atoms of uranium change in an atomic reactor, or atoms of hydrogen in a bomb, or in the sun.

Heat is made by **friction**, when two rough surfaces rub together.

Here is a third way to make heat. When an electric current passes through a wire the wire gets hot. These things give heat because in them is a wire or wires that get hot when an electric current passes through:

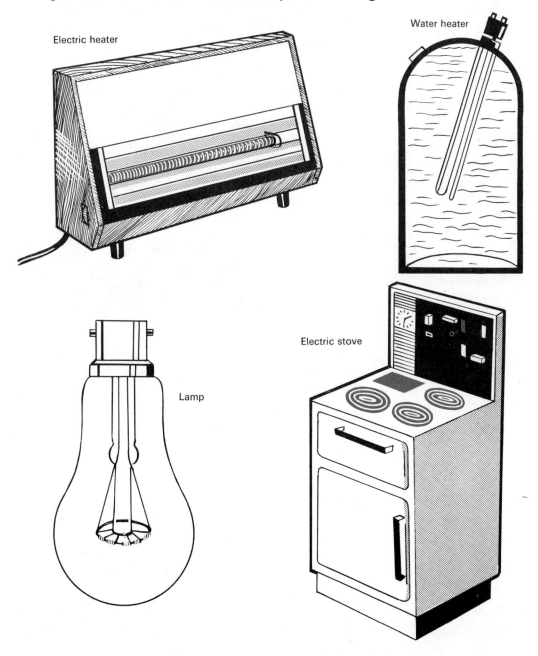

Electric heater

Water heater

Lamp

Electric stove

Chapter 5

How heat travels

This ice-cream is gaining heat

This hot tea is losing heat

The cup of tea is cooling down and the ice-cream is getting warm. **Hot** things are always **losing** heat to colder things around them, while **cold** things are always **gaining** heat from warmer things around them.

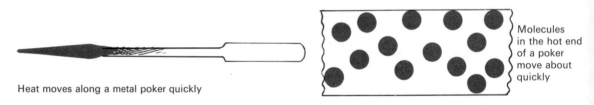

Heat moves along a metal poker quickly

Molecules in the hot end of a poker move about quickly

Heat travels from one thing to another in three ways. One end of the poker is in the fire but the other end soon gets hot as well. The molecules in the hot end move about very quickly and bump into the molecules next to them. These start to move quickly and bump into the next ones and so on right along the poker. When heat moves in this way we say it travels by **conduction**.

Wood will burn, but heat does not move quickly along it

If you hold one end of a stick in the fire you can hold the other end until the flames nearly reach your fingers. Heat does not travel easily along wood: we say that wood is a **bad conductor**. Glass, brick, pottery, rubber, wool, fur, plastics, air and water are all **bad conductors** of heat. Metals conduct heat well. We say they are **good conductors**.

A saucepan is made of metal so that heat travels easily through to the water. Its handle is made of wood or hardened rubber so that it keeps cool.

This saucepan has a thick flat bottom

Which foot in the next drawing will feel the colder? The metal conducts heat away easily. It is very smooth so that nearly every part of the sole of the foot touches the metal. The foot on the metal will feel very cold.

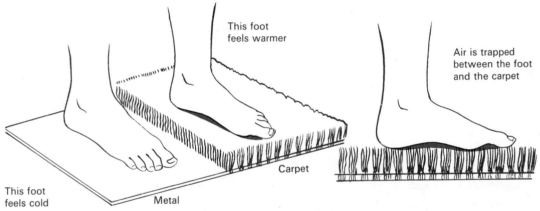

This foot feels warmer

Air is trapped between the foot and the carpet

This foot feels cold

Metal

Carpet

The wool carpet does not conduct the heat away easily. It is rough, so quite a lot of air is trapped between the sole of the foot and the carpet. This foot feels quite warm.

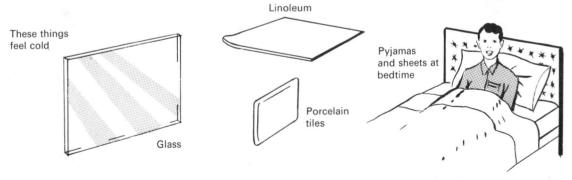

These things feel cold

Linoleum

Glass

Porcelain tiles

Pyjamas and sheets at bedtime

Metals conduct heat away easily, so they feel cold. Smooth things feel colder than rough. When things are smooth, much more of the surfaces touch and much less air is trapped. Have you noticed how cold newly ironed sheets and pyjamas feel at bedtime?

Good conductors warm up more quickly and cool down more quickly than bad conductors. You can show this at the seaside. When you go bathing on a hot sunny afternoon, the sand feels hot but the sea feels cold. If you go midnight bathing you will notice that the water feels warmer than the sand.

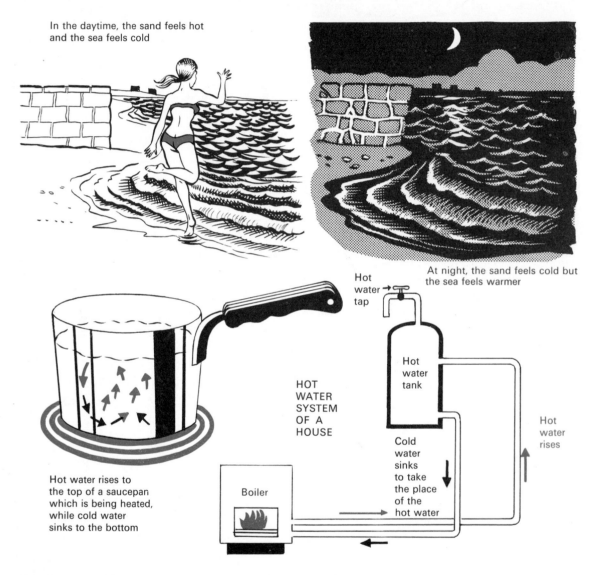

In the daytime, the sand feels hot and the sea feels cold

At night, the sand feels cold but the sea feels warmer

Hot water rises to the top of a saucepan which is being heated, while cold water sinks to the bottom

HOT WATER SYSTEM OF A HOUSE

Hot water tap

Hot water tank

Boiler

Cold water sinks to take the place of the hot water

Hot water rises

We have said that water is a very poor conductor. In that case, how does the water at the top of the saucepan get hot so quickly? Hot water is lighter than cold (see page 10), so the water heated in a saucepan moves as you see in the drawing. In your house, the hot water system works because hot water rises. The radiators in your classroom heat all the air in the room because **hot air rises** and **cold air sinks** to take its place.

24

HEAT

A coal fire is very wasteful. The room is drafty, but the air is fresh. Modern fireplaces cut out drafts, and some of the hot air is sent back into the room. When heat travels because hot air or water move, we say the heat travels by **convection**.

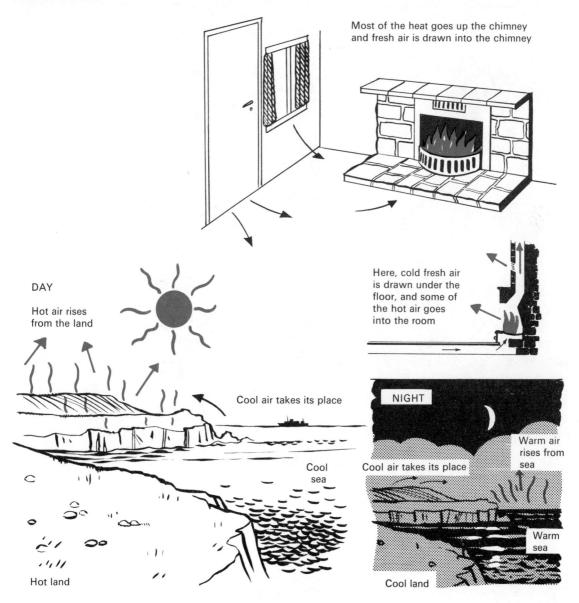

Most of the heat goes up the chimney and fresh air is drawn into the chimney

Here, cold fresh air is drawn under the floor, and some of the hot air goes into the room

DAY

Hot air rises from the land

Cool air takes its place

Cool sea

Hot land

NIGHT

Warm air rises from sea

Cool air takes its place

Warm sea

Cool land

The movement of air or water is called a **convection current**. Some winds are convection currents.

Gliders and birds use hot rising air (called thermals) to carry them higher into the air.

Chapter 6

The Sun

The screen stops rays from reaching the boy, and the shiny side will reflect them back into the fire

The boy in the picture is warming his hands in front of the fire. The heat does not reach his hands either by convection or by conduction. Rays of heat travel from the fire in straight lines. We say the heat travels by **radiation**. He cannot feel the heat in the next picture, because the fire screen stops the rays of heat. If the fire screen is a shiny, light-colored one, most of the heat rays bounce back towards the fire. We say the rays are **reflected**.

You can keep cool in the shade of a tree

In hot countries, buildings are painted white because white reflects the heat

The shiny reflector behind an electric heater reflects the heat rays. If the fire screen is a dull black one, most of the rays go into the fire screen and it becomes very hot—we say the rays are **absorbed**.

The sun's heat reaches the earth by radiation. Heat rays from the sun travel through ninety-three million miles of space to the earth. Because these rays travel in straight lines you can keep cool in the shade of a tree.

HEAT

White clothes and white houses reflect some of the sun's rays. Dark clothes and buildings absorb most of the rays. In hot countries, buildings are painted white and clothes are light-colored because they are cooler.

The air is heated only a little as the rays travel through. When they reach the dull brown earth and rocks they are absorbed. The soil and rocks become hot, and the air near the ground is heated and rises.

Water vapor and clouds act like a blanket. They stop some of the heat from reaching the ground so on a cloudy day it warms up more slowly. They also stop some of the heat from leaving the ground so it cools more slowly on cloudy nights. On dry summer days and in the deserts of the world the ground gets hot very quickly, so the days are very hot but very soon after sunset the ground loses its heat quickly. Nights in the Sahara Desert can be very cold. Clear dry winter nights are usually frosty. Frost seldom forms on cloudy nights.

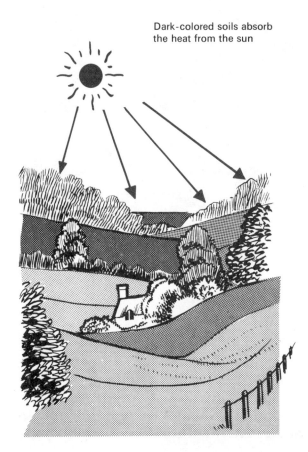

Dark-colored soils absorb the heat from the sun

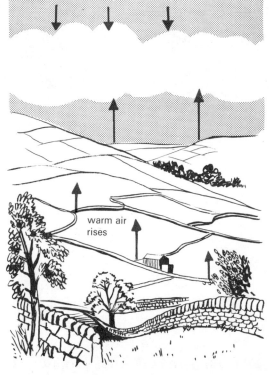

Clouds prevent some heat from reaching the earth and also prevent its escaping from the earth

warm air rises

You can use a lens to make the sun's rays set fire to a piece of paper. Glass bottles thrown onto dry grass, or a goldfish bowl standing in a sunny window, can start a fire. The heat rays from the sun can be reflected. In ancient times huge curved brass mirrors were used to start fires.

The pictures show an Egyptian sun engine used to turn water into steam, and a solar furnace (solar means sun). In the furnace, the place where the sun's rays are brought together is about thirty times as hot as boiling water.

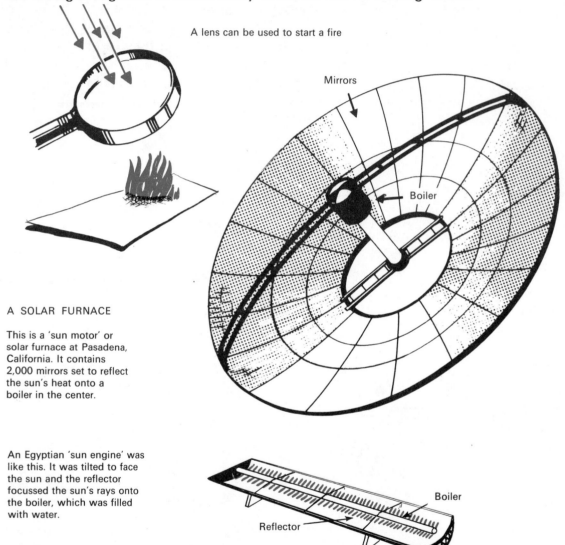

A lens can be used to start a fire

A SOLAR FURNACE

This is a 'sun motor' or solar furnace at Pasadena, California. It contains 2,000 mirrors set to reflect the sun's heat onto a boiler in the center.

An Egyptian 'sun engine' was like this. It was tilted to face the sun and the reflector focussed the sun's rays onto the boiler, which was filled with water.

Heat travels by conduction, convection and radiation. Very often, however, we want to stop heat from traveling.

When we want to stop a thing from losing or gaining heat, we cover it with something that does not conduct heat easily. We **insulate** it.

HEAT

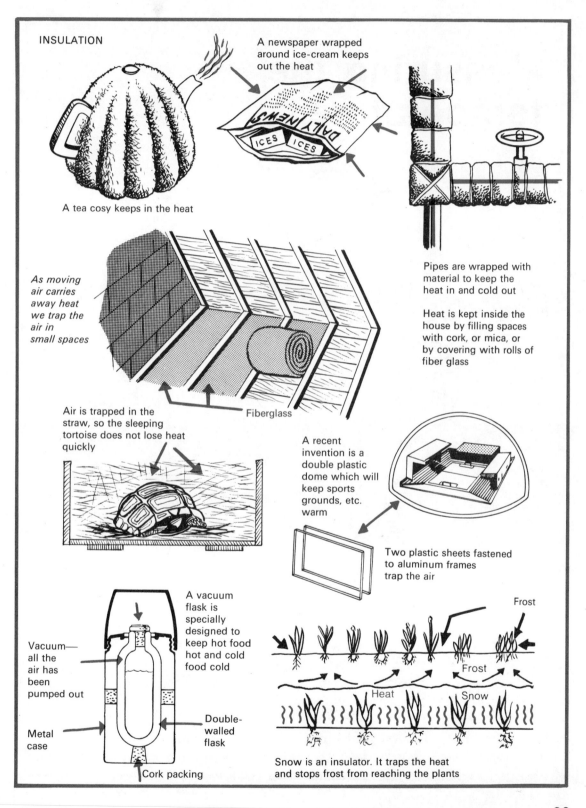

INSULATION

A tea cosy keeps in the heat

A newspaper wrapped around ice-cream keeps out the heat

DAILY NEWS

ICES ICES

Pipes are wrapped with material to keep the heat in and cold out

Heat is kept inside the house by filling spaces with cork, or mica, or by covering with rolls of fiber glass

As moving air carries away heat we trap the air in small spaces

Fiberglass

Air is trapped in the straw, so the sleeping tortoise does not lose heat quickly

A recent invention is a double plastic dome which will keep sports grounds, etc. warm

Two plastic sheets fastened to aluminum frames trap the air

A vacuum flask is specially designed to keep hot food hot and cold food cold

Vacuum—all the air has been pumped out

Metal case

Double-walled flask

Cork packing

Frost

Frost

Heat

Snow

Snow is an insulator. It traps the heat and stops frost from reaching the plants

Chapter 7

Measuring the temperature

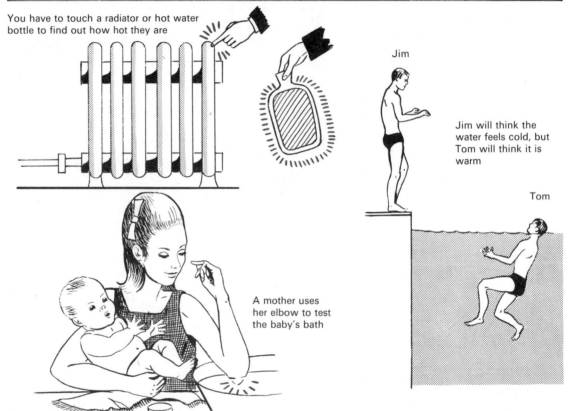

You have to touch a radiator or hot water bottle to find out how hot they are

Jim

Jim will think the water feels cold, but Tom will think it is warm

Tom

A mother uses her elbow to test the baby's bath

You can **see** when a fire is burning or when an electric or gas heater is turned **on** but you have to **touch** a radiator pipe or hot water bottle to find out how hot it is. Can you tell accurately how hot something is by touching it? The two boys in the picture jump into the swimming pool. Jim has been under the hot shower. Tom has been under the cold shower. Jim will think the water feels cold, but Tom will think the water feels warm.

Your mother is used to putting her hands into very hot water for washing and cleaning, so she has to use her elbow to test the baby's bath water. Touch the wooden and metal parts of your desk. They are both about as warm as the air around them, but the metal **feels** much colder. You should now know why.

Many years ago scientists realized that something more accurate than touch was needed to measure **temperature**; that is, how hot a thing is.

The first picture on this page shows the first **thermometer** ('therm' means heat; 'meter' means measure). It was made in 1592 by Galileo. About 50 years later, a Frenchman called Rey made a water thermometer. You can see this in the second picture.

At the beginning of the eighteenth century mercury was used instead of water. In 1714 a German scientist called Fahrenheit realized that for the thermometer to be of any use a scale that everyone could read was needed. He mixed salt and ice together and put his thermometer in the mixture. He marked the level of the mercury in the thermometer as 0. He put the thermometer on his body and marked the new level as 100. (We now know that the body temperature is usually 98·4°F.) On his scale the freezing point of water is 32 and the boiling point 212.

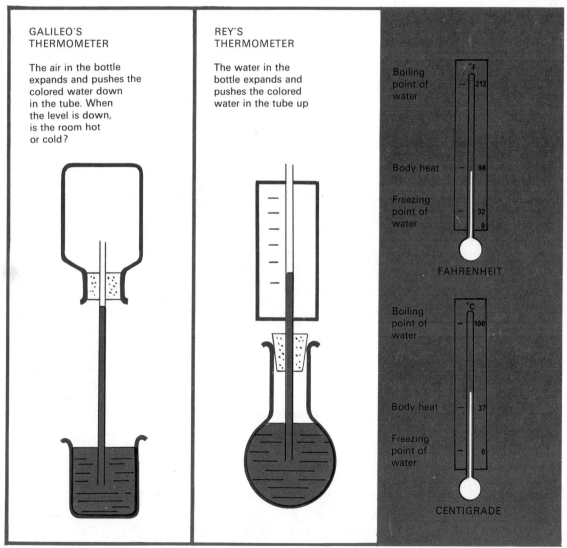

GALILEO'S
THERMOMETER

The air in the bottle
expands and pushes the
colored water down
in the tube. When
the level is down,
is the room hot
or cold?

REY'S
THERMOMETER

The water in the
bottle expands and
pushes the colored
water in the tube up

Boiling
point of
water

Body heat

Freezing
point of
water

°F
212

98

32
0

FAHRENHEIT

Boiling
point of
water

Body heat

Freezing
point of
water

°C
100

37

0

CENTIGRADE

In 1742 Celsius, a Swedish scientist, made another scale with the freezing point of water 0° and the boiling point 100°. This scale is called the **centigrade** scale ('cent' means 100). It is now used by scientists all over the world.

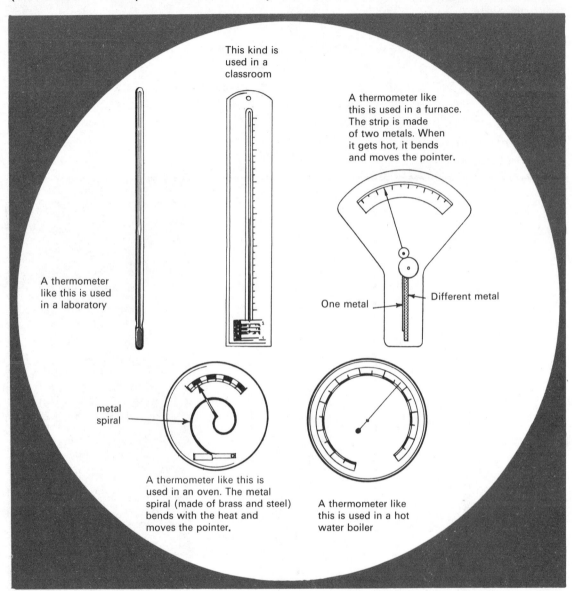

This kind is used in a classroom

A thermometer like this is used in a furnace. The strip is made of two metals. When it gets hot, it bends and moves the pointer.

A thermometer like this is used in a laboratory

One metal

Different metal

metal spiral

A thermometer like this is used in an oven. The metal spiral (made of brass and steel) bends with the heat and moves the pointer.

A thermometer like this is used in a hot water boiler

In the United States, the Fahrenheit scale is most widely used. Scientists, who work generally with the Centigrade scale, tell us that the lowest temperature is −273°C., but in special laboratories the lowest temperature they have been able to obtain is just under −272°C. At −273°C. the molecules are quite still. There are several kinds of thermometers. On this page are pictures of some of them.

When you are ill the doctor puts a special thermometer into your mouth for about half a minute. He takes it out and reads your temperature. (The little kink in the tube stops the mercury from going back down the tube until he shakes it.) If you are well, your temperature will read about 98·4°F. When you are ill, your temperature may be higher or lower than this, but human body temperature seldom rises above 107°F. or falls below 96°F.

Your temperature normally remains the same whether the day is hot (95°F.), or cold (25°F.); whether you are in a hot bath (105°F.), or in a cold one (55°F.).

CLINICAL THERMOMETER

Notice that the inner tube has a kink, and that the numbers go from 95 to 108

Chapter 8

Heat, cold– and our bodies

Bread

Rice

Sugar

You breathe in the oxygen in the air

Potatoes

Your body has its own **heating system**. It needs **fuel** and **oxygen**. In the picture are some of the body's fuels. You get the oxygen from the air when you breathe in. When any part of your body does anything—when your leg kicks, your brain thinks, or your eye blinks—the fuel and oxygen join together and give energy and heat. Your blood carries the fuel and oxygen to every part of the body. When you play football or basketball you need more oxygen and fuel— you breathe quickly, you grow hungry and you become very **hot**.

Your body also needs a **cooling system**, and all over your skin there are little holes called pores. When you are hot, these holes open to let out water mixed with salt (sweat). As sweat evaporates it takes heat from the body. This cooling system is so good than men can work in front of white-hot furnaces or in the hottest regions of the world. But because such workingmen may lose three or four gallons of sweat in a day, they have to drink a great deal of water and take special salt tablets. (Look carefully at the drawing of the skin on the opposite page.)

HEAT

In a hot stuffy room people often faint. The air is so full of water vapor that the sweat does not evaporate, and so the body becomes overheated. On a very hot day in summer a breeze feels cool and refreshing because the sweat evaporates easily. Athletes always do as you see in the picture after an event so that the body does not cool too rapidly.

When you are hot your face becomes very red. This is caused by the blood rushing to your skin to get cool. When you are very cold you turn blue. Then, the blood rushes away from your skin. When you shiver, some of your muscles move quickly to make heat.

Joan can go out in the sun for a longer time than Mary. Under her skin is a layer of coloring called **pigment**. This absorbs the heat from the sun. Mary has very little pigment and so she quickly burns and blisters. To stop the heat from the sun Mary covers her skin with a suntan cream or lotion.

THE SKIN

Hairs

The pores open when you are hot

Athletes put on a track suit before and after an event to keep warm

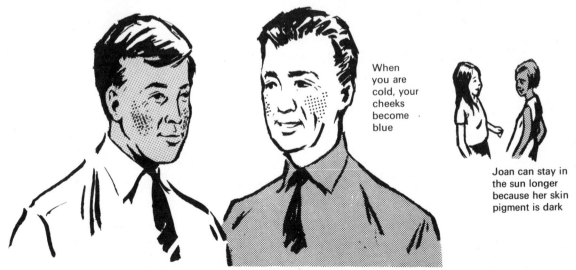

Your face becomes red when you are hot

When you are cold, your cheeks become blue

Joan can stay in the sun longer because her skin pigment is dark

John does not dither on the edge of the water like Bill. He has a thick layer of fat under his skin. Fat is a good **insulator** and so his body does not cool down as quickly as Bill's. Bill has only a very thin layer of fat, but on hot days Bill can keep much cooler than John.

Whales, seals, walruses and penguins have very thick layers of fat that keep them warm in Arctic waters. Channel swimmers cover their bodies with thick layers of grease to keep out the cold. A camel has all his fat in one place, so that his body keeps cool.

Bill is thin

John is fat

Mary's skin is fair, so she burns easily

Channel swimmers cover themselves with grease

Seals are fat

In hot countries or on a hot summer's day, the body loses very little heat to the air around, so people often do not wear much clothing. In colder countries, the body loses a great deal of heat, so people wear **insulators**.

36

HEAT

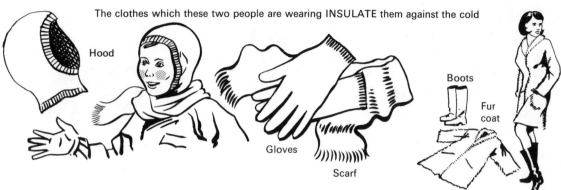

The clothes which these two people are wearing INSULATE them against the cold

Hood

Gloves

Scarf

Boots

Fur coat

A newly born baby has to be warmly wrapped up all the time but as she grows older, her body has to learn to live in different temperatures. Some children are dressed in too many clothes all the time, so their bodies never learn to do this and they catch cold and chills very easily. With modern air travel, man's body has to learn to be very adaptable. Man is known as a **warm-blooded** animal.

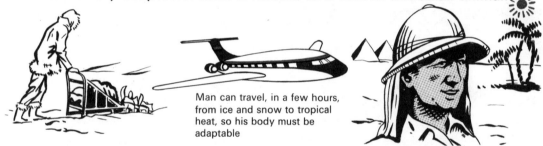

Man can travel, in a few hours, from ice and snow to tropical heat, so his body must be adaptable

Animals that live where it is hot all the year round have very little fur:

Elephant

Giraffe

Camel

Animals that live where it is cold all the year round have very thick fur:

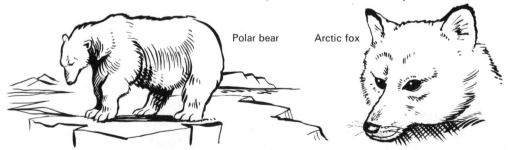

Polar bear

Arctic fox

37

Some animals and birds live where it is hot in summer and cold in winter:

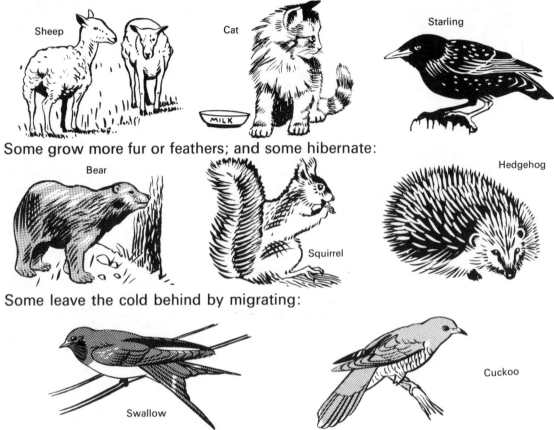

Sheep

Cat

Starling

Some grow more fur or feathers; and some hibernate:

Bear

Squirrel

Hedgehog

Some leave the cold behind by migrating:

Swallow

Cuckoo

The animals in the next pictures are called **cold-blooded**, because their bodies are the same temperature as their surroundings. Most of the reptiles hibernate in cold weather. Many of the insects are killed by the cold but some do live through the winter.

Frog

Snake

Tortoise

Horsefly's eggs

Butterfly's chrysalis

Some insects sleep crowded together in tiny crevices

HEAT

Most plants rest through the cold winter and many trees lose their leaves. Some plants die down to ground level but the roots live on through the winter. They become swollen with stored food and when spring and the warmer weather comes, the roots sprout again. Can you find out what bulbs, corms and tubers are? How do they differ?

Some plants die altogether but their little dry seeds live on. They can survive in frozen ground since there is no water in them to freeze.

Just as you feel most comfortable when the temperature is about 60°F. to 70°F. (15° − 20°C.), so most living things, plants and animals, have a certain temperature that suits them best. A polar bear and penguin thrive where it is very cold, a crocodile and giraffe where it is very hot. Wheat grows best at 77°F. (25°C.), and a cucumber at 86°F. (30°C.). A gardener will tell you that some plants need shade, some the hot sun, and some will only live in a greenhouse in cooler countries. That is why plant and animal life varies in the different climates of the world.

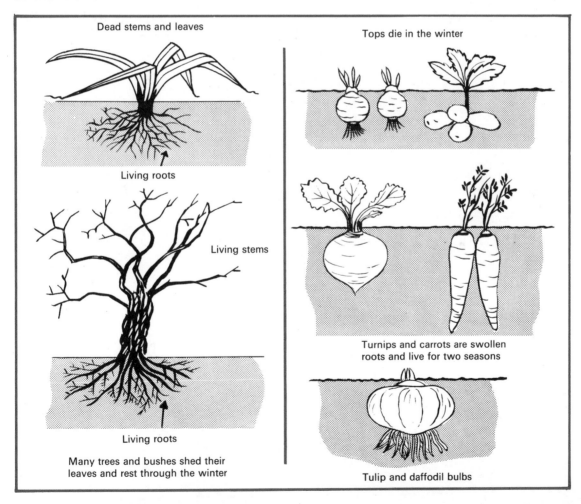

Dead stems and leaves

Tops die in the winter

Living roots

Living stems

Living roots

Many trees and bushes shed their leaves and rest through the winter

Turnips and carrots are swollen roots and live for two seasons

Tulip and daffodil bulbs

Chapter 9

Man uses heat and cold

[1] For comfort.   Rooms can be kept at a comfortable temperature (60°F. – 70 °F. or 15°C. – 20°C.) by heaters and radiators when it is cold. Hot-water bottles and electric blankets keep man's bed warm.

[2] For cleaning.   Hot water melts grease; things dissolve more easily in hot water than cold.

[3] For drying and ironing.

[4] For improving food. Most foods taste better and are more easily digested when cooked with the right amount of heat. Too much heat spoils food. **The black burnt part is carbon**. Meat is softened and the fat melted so that most of it runs out. Fruit and vegetables are softened.

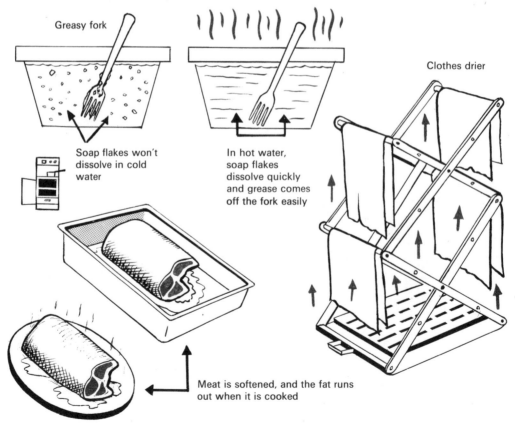

Greasy fork

Soap flakes won't dissolve in cold water

In hot water, soap flakes dissolve quickly and grease comes off the fork easily

Clothes drier

Meat is softened, and the fat runs out when it is cooked

Heat changes food. Sugar becomes a brown liquid; then sets like toffee. Starchy things when heated in water become gluey. Flour and water make thick gravy, cornflour makes custard or pie fillings, rice and sago make thick milk puddings.

Eggs become hard. Liquids evaporate. A baked cake tastes better than a raw one. You cannot brew tea or coffee with cold water. Some foods taste better when frozen or chilled, such as ice-cream, fruit juices and jelly.

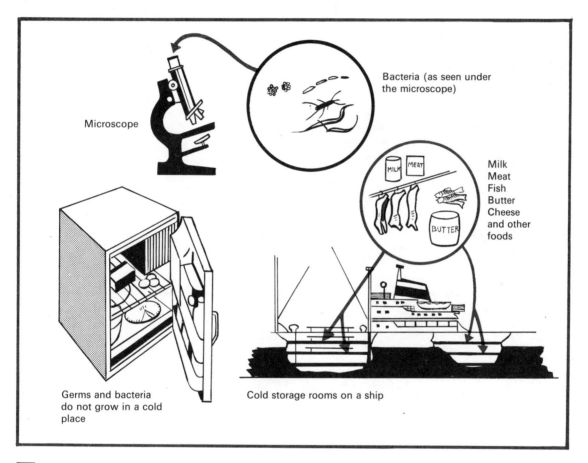

Microscope

Bacteria (as seen under the microscope)

Milk
Meat
Fish
Butter
Cheese
and other
foods

Germs and bacteria do not grow in a cold place

Cold storage rooms on a ship

5 For preventing food from going bad. In all food there are germs and bacteria. If they grow and multiply, the food goes bad. To do this they need warmth and moisture.

In a cold place like a refrigerator the germs and bacteria cannot grow, but they are not killed. Food kept in a refrigerator does not go bad, but as soon as it is brought out, the bacteria start to grow and the food begins to decay.

Food cargo ships have refrigerated holds. Most food shops have refrigerators. You can now buy frozen foods of all kinds—meat, fish, fruit, vegetables, even cakes and pastry.

When food is heated to 100 °C. or 212 °F., the bacteria that make the food go bad are killed. If the hot food is then sealed in a tin or jar, so that no new bacteria in the air can reach it, the food does not go bad.

When milk is **pasteurized**, it is heated to 150 °F. (67 °C) for 30 minutes. This kills all the harmful germs in it that cause disease. It tastes like fresh milk and does go sour.

When milk is **sterilized** it is boiled. This kills all the germs and the bacteria, so in sealed bottles or tins it does not go sour. The taste is different.

Food is sealed in tin cans and jars after heating   Pasteurized and Sterilized milk

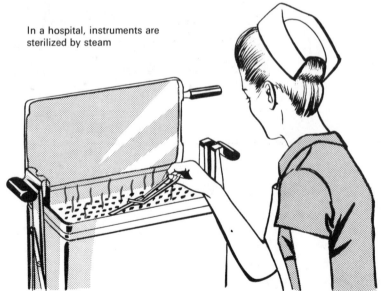

In a hospital, instruments are sterilized by steam

6 To kill germs. In hospitals, and in doctors' and dentists' offices, all instruments are heated with steam in a **sterilizer** to kill germs and bacteria.

7 In industry.   In all kinds of factories and workshops heat is used for different things. Find out how, and why, heat is used in the industries in your town. Some things are heated to give other things. Iron ore and coke are heated to give iron. Coal is heated to give coal gas, tar, coke, oil, sulfur and many other things. Some things need to be heated so that they can be shaped or moulded, such as metals, plastic, wood.

8 Heat is used to make power. Water is heated to make steam. The steam drives turbines in electric power stations, in ships and in all kinds of factories. Heat is used to cause explosions in quarrying and mining and for various purposes in warfare.

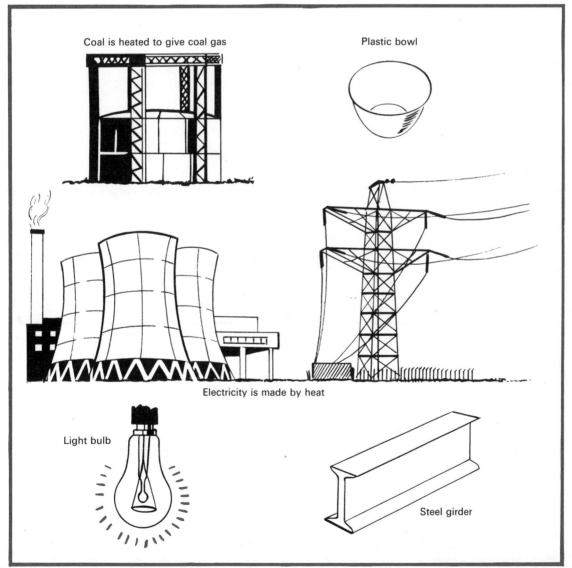

Coal is heated to give coal gas

Plastic bowl

Electricity is made by heat

Light bulb

Steel girder

The first steam turbine was made by a man called Hero in Alexandria over 2000 years ago. Here are instructions for making a model steam engine like Hero's.

1. Take an empty syrup can.

2. Drill 2 small holes, one on each side of the can, about an inch or more from the top.

3. Bend two narrow copper tubes to right angles and solder them into the holes.

4. Drill a hole in the center of the top of the can, and another of the same size in the center of the bottom.

5. Put a piece of copper tubing, the same size in diameter as the hole and slightly longer than the can, in a vise and nip $1\frac{1}{2}$ inches from the top.

6. Push this tubing through the can and solder it in place.

7. Push a long piece of thick steel wire into a block of wood.

8. Place a very small test tube over the end of the wire, then push this into the copper tubing which is through the tin can.

To use the engine, pour water very carefully down one of the narrow bent tubes, then heat it.

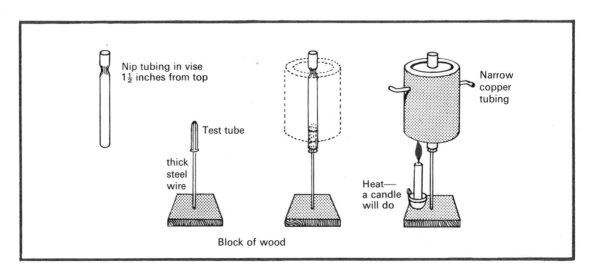

Nip tubing in vise
$1\frac{1}{2}$ inches from top

Test tube

thick
steel
wire

Narrow
copper
tubing

Heat—
a candle
will do

Block of wood

Chapter 10

What is heat?

It is not a solid, a liquid or a gas. Heat cannot be weighed. A piece of metal weighs the same whether it is hot or cold. You cannot buy a bottle of heat, but heat can **do** things. In science when anything is moved, we say that **work** has been done and **energy** has been used to move it. Heat moves the cork out of the bottle. Heat is **energy**.

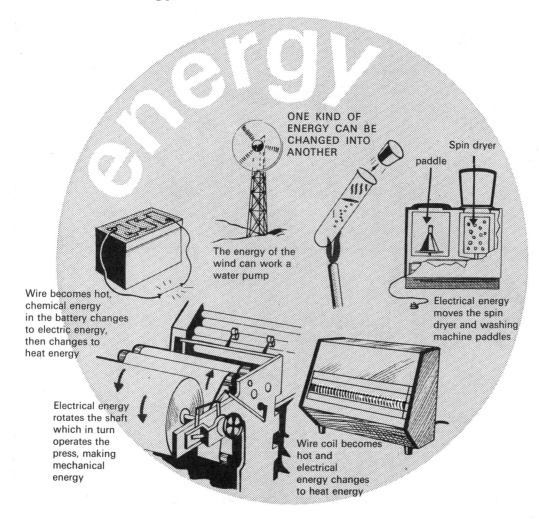

The pictures show some things being moved by different kinds of energy. Where does all this energy come from?

To live and grow, a plant must have food. It uses the light rays from the sun to make its food. Light energy from the sun makes plants grow. Animals and man eat plants (or animals that have eaten plants) to give them energy so that they can move and work. Man burns fuels to make steam power to move his machines, engines and generators to make electricity. But you have read that all fuels come from plants or animals.

If you think very carefully you will find that energy can be traced back to the sun.

Man eats plants and is given energy

Light energy makes plants grow

1 The sun gives light energy . . .

2 . . . to make plants grow . . .

3 . . . to form coal . . .

4 . . . to burn and give heat energy to turn water . . .

5 . . . into steam energy

6 . . . to run a turbine . . .

7 . . . which turns a dynamo

8 Electric energy is made . . .

9 . . . which is turned into light energy

Chapter 11

Some important facts

1 Heat is a form of **energy**.

2 Heat is made by **friction** when two surfaces rub together.

3 Heat is made when one thing changes into another:

(*a*) when something burns, joining with the oxygen in the air to make a different substance.

(*b*) in damp hayricks when hay decays.

(*c*) when water is mixed with quicklime to make slaked lime.

(*d*) when the atom of one thing changes into the atom of another, in the **sun**, in a nuclear reactor or in an atomic bomb.

4 Heat is made when an electric current passes through a wire.

5 When something is heated, its molecules move very quickly.

6 If you **heat** most **solids**, they become **liquids**, then **gases**.

7 If you cool most gases, they become **liquids**, then **solids**.

8 Heat makes most solids, liquids and gases **expand**.

9 Most solids, liquids and gases **contract** when cooled.

10 Heat travels: it passes from something hot to something cooler. It travels by:

(*a*) **Radiation**. Rays of heat travel in straight lines, through space or air.

(*b*) **Convection**, when hot air or liquids rise.

(*c*) **Conduction**, when heat travels along a solid.

11 We **insulate** something to stop heat traveling to it or from it.

12 The level of heat (**temperature**) is measured by a **thermometer**.

13 Animals and plants rely mainly on the **sun** for heating their surroundings.

14 A warm-blooded animal (including man) has its own heating and cooling system so that its body is always at about the same temperature.

15 A warm-blooded animal keeps its body warm by exercise (for this it needs **food** and **oxygen**) and by its covering of fat, and fur or feathers (man wears clothes).

16 It keeps cool by sweating.

17 A cold-blooded animal is the same temperature as its surroundings.

18 For each plant or animal there is a temperature that suits it best. The plant or animal dies if left in a temperature much above or below this.

19 Man uses heat for comfort, for cleaning, for drying and ironing, for improving and keeping his food, for killing germs and bacteria. He uses heat in industry, for smelting, moulding, and so on, and to make power—including steam, electric power and atomic power.